CONTINENTS OF THE WORLD

ASIA

Rob Bowden

WORLD ALMANAC® LIBRARY

Please visit our web site at: www.worldalmanaclibrary.com
For a free color catalog describing World Almanac® Library's list of high-quality books and multimedia programs, call 1-800-848-2928 (USA) or 1-800-387-3178 (Canada). World Almanac® Library's fax: (414) 332-3567.

Library of Congress Cataloging-in-Publication Data

Bowden, Rob.
    Asia / by Rob Bowden.
      p. cm. — (Continents of the world)
    Includes bibliographical references and index.
    ISBN 0-8368-5911-1 (lib. bdg.)
    ISBN 0-8368-5918-9 (softcover)
    1. Asia—Juvenile literature. I. Title. II. Continents of the
world (Milwaukee, Wis.)
  DS5.B57   2005
  915—dc22   2005042111

This North American edition first published in 2006 by
World Almanac® Library
330 West Olive Street, Suite 100
Milwaukee, WI 53212 USA

Commissioning editor: Victoria Brooker
Editor: Kelly Davis
Inside design: Jane Hawkins
Series concept and project management by
EASI-Educational Resourcing, (info@easi-er.co.uk)
Statistical research: Anna Bowden
World Almanac® Library editor: Barbara Kiely Miller
World Almanac® Library art direction: Tammy West
World Almanac® Library cover design: Dave Kowalski
World Almanac® Library production: Jessica Morris

Photo credits: Chris Fairclough Worldwide: 4, 9, 45(t); Christine Osborne Pictures 39; Corbis cover, 6 (Yann Arthus-Bertrand), 7 (Michael S. Yamashita), 8 (Araldo de Luca), 11 (Robert Essel NYC), 12 (Bettmann), 13 (Ahmad Masood/Reuters), 14, 34(t) (Macduff Everton), 15 (Kimimasa Mayama/Reuters), 16 (Michael S. Yamashita), 17 (David Turnley), 18, 20(t) (Wolfgang Kaehler), 22 (Bohemian Nomad Picturemakers), 23 (Shepard Sherbell/Corbis Saba), 24 (Howard Davies) 28 (Alison Wright), 29 (Beawiharta/Reuters), 30 (Liu Liqun), 33(b) (Kimimasa Mayama/Reuters), 35 (Max Rossi/Reuters), 36 (The Cover Story), 37 (Peter Blakely/Corbis Saba), 38 (Colin Garratt), 42 (Ed Kashi), 44 (Jose Fuste Raga), 45(b) (Jagadeesh Nv/Reuters), 48 (East/Reuters), 49 (Langevin Jacques/Corbis Sygma), 19, 50, 51, 58 (Reuters), 53 (Jeremy Horner), 54, 59 (Keren Su), 55 (D. Robert and Lorri Fran), 56 (Theo Allofs); EASI-Images/Tony Binns 1, 3, 10(b), 25, 26, 40, 47, 52; Rob Bowden 34(b), 20(b), 27, 33(t), 41, 43, 46, 57; Roy Maconachie 31; Miguel Hunt 32; Mary Evans Picture Library 10(t). Maps and graphs: Martin Darlison, Encompass Graphics. Population Distribution Map © 2003 UT-Battelle, LLC.

Printed in China

1 2 3 4 5 6 7 8 9 09 08 07 06 05

The skyline of Hong Kong is just one symbol of Asia's emergence as a global economic center during the twentieth century.

CONTENTS

ASIA — THE LAND OF PEOPLE

Asia's fifty countries make up a vast continent of about 17,568,000 square miles (45,500,000 square kilometers), or 34 percent of the world's total land area. It stretches from Europe in the west to Japan in the east and almost reaches Australia in the southeast. Asia also includes the predominantly Arab nations of the Middle East and the majority of Russia, the world's largest country.

The most striking thing about Asia is its enormous population. In 2003, Asia accounted for almost two-thirds of the world's population—an incredible 4 billion people. China alone had a population of 1.3 billion, with India not far behind with 1.1 billion people. Asia is home to hundreds of distinct ethnic groups, ranging from the Chukchi and Nenet who live in Russia's frozen Arctic to the Karen and Hanunoo who inhabit the tropics of Southeast Asia.

Asia's landscapes include the world's highest mountain range, the Himalayas, and several major deserts, including the Gobi and Arabian deserts. Many of the world's largest rivers, including the Yangtze, Ganges, Indus, and Mekong, are also found in Asia. In the far east, Asia becomes a continent of islands. Some are large, such as the main islands of Japan and Indonesia, but this region has countless smaller islands, with about 13,600 in Indonesia alone.

Economically, Asia is becoming one of the world's most powerful regions. Japan has by far the largest economy (second to the United States in global terms), but China is catching up fast. Since the early 1990s, it

Shanghai, with about 12.7 million people, is the largest city in China, the world's most populous country.

has been one of the world's fastest-growing economies, with an annual growth rate averaging nearly 10 percent between 1991 and 2002. The oil-rich countries of the Middle East, such as Saudi Arabia and Kuwait, are also important economically and play a key role in global energy supplies. In stark contrast, Asia also has some of the world's poorest countries where life for many is a daily struggle against disease and malnutrition. These countries include Afghanistan, Bangladesh, and Nepal.

Asia has the potential to become the world's most important continent in the twenty-first century both politically and economically. Optimism for its future is marred, however, by ongoing tensions and conflicts from Israel and the Palestinians in the west to North and South Korea in the east.

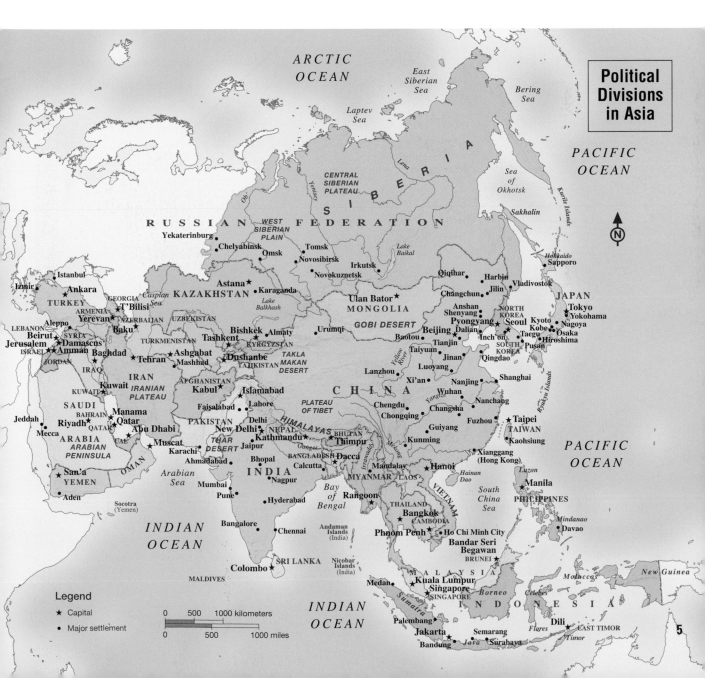

Political Divisions in Asia

Legend
★ Capital
• Major settlement

0   500   1000 kilometers

0   500   1000 miles

1. THE HISTORY OF ASIA

MANY OF THE THINGS THAT WE TAKE FOR GRANTED TODAY EMERGED out of Asia's long and complex history. Asians are thought to have been the first to domesticate plants and animals in about 8000 B.C. This development enabled people to engage in activities other than hunting and gathering for the first time, and as a result, some of the first known human settlements emerged in Jericho (Israeli-controlled West Bank) and Catal Huyuk (Turkey). Since those early days, Asia has played a prominent role in world history from early civilizations and great empires to major wars and groundbreaking achievements.

EARLY SETTLEMENT

The earliest evidence of human life in Asia is found in western China and the Indonesian island of Java. In both locations, the remains of *Homo erectus* (an early ancestor of modern humans) have been found that date back 1.7 to 1.3 million years. Basic stone tools and evidence of the use of fire were also discovered. Other remains dating back about 0.6 million years have been found in Vietnam, Thailand, and Korea.

Archaeologists excavate the remains of an early human settlement at Catal Huyuk in Turkey. The settlement is thought to date back to 7000 B.C.

The first modern humans (*Homo sapiens sapiens*) arrived in western Asia from Africa about 100,000 years ago and from there spread eastward, reaching Japan about 50,000 years ago and northern Siberia about 30,000 years ago. Asia also

The ziggurat of Ur was the centerpiece of the ancient Sumerian city of Ur in modern-day Iraq. It was built as a temple to the moon god Nanna.

acted as the corridor for the expansion of modern humans into the Americas from across the Bering Strait about 15,000 years ago and into Australia about 50,000 years ago.

FIRST CIVILIZATIONS

About 3500 B.C., agriculture in the Tigris and Euphrates river valleys (an area known as Mesopotamia) had become so successful that wealthy individuals and families began to divert labor and resources into building impressive ceremonial temples. The buildings became the focus for the world's first known civilization—the Sumerians—in the area that is now Iraq. Farming communities gathered around these temples, and small villages turned into organized cities and centers of trade and craft. Lagosh, Uruk, Umma, and Ur were among the most significant of these cities. The success of the Sumerians and later Mesopotamian cultures depended on their ability to redirect water from the Tigris and Euphrates rivers to their fields through a system of irrigation canals. This same factor was central to one of Asia's other early civilizations in the Indus river valley of Pakistan.

Agricultural towns first appeared in the Indus valley about 3500 B.C., but it was not until 2500 B.C. that a major civilization emerged. Mohenjo-Daro was one of the key cities of the Indus valley civilization. Archaeological finds show that besides farming, it had well-established trade links with

FACT FILE

The earliest evidence of farming comes from the Levant (modern-day Israel, Lebanon, Syria, and Turkey) and dates back 10,000 years. Farming in China developed independently between 8,000 and 9,000 years ago.

FACT FILE

The Silk Road—a trade route that connected cities in the Far East with those in the Middle East, Europe, and Africa—came into existence in about 100 B.C. It is one of the oldest trade routes in the world.

Mesopotamia and ancient Egypt. This advanced civilization collapsed about 2000 B.C. for reasons that are not fully known. The most likely explanation is that the collapse was the result of a change in the course of the Indus river.

In China, the Shang civilization emerged about 1800 B.C. and remained a major power for about seven hundred years. The Shang dynasty does not appear to have developed extensive trade networks. Skilled craftsmanship, however, especially in bronze and lacquer work, did emerge as one of the Shang dynasty's main characteristics.

AGE OF EMPIRE

By about 1000 B.C., several of Asia's early civilizations had become super-states with powerful armies. This development marked an age of empire and warfare as successive Asian societies fought for control over large areas of the continent. The Assyrians were one of the first great empires, and from their capital in today's northern Iraq, they managed to unite and control much of western Asia for the first time. Subsequent empires followed, including the Babylonians and the Persians. One of the most famous, though short-lived, empires was that of Alexander the Great. An outstanding military general, he led the Greek army in the defeat of the Persians and gained control of large parts of western and central Asia between 334 and 323 B.C.

This detail from a mosaic originally located in the ancient city of Pompeii shows Alexander the Great as a great warrior during the Battle of Issus in 333 B.C. Alexander won the battle, defeating the Persian King Darius.

CHANGE AND DIVISION

The period from 300 B.C. to A.D. 1600 saw dramatic changes across Asia. In about 221 B.C., China emerged as a unified state under its first emperor, Qin Shi Huangdi. The Mauryan empire (325–185 B.C.) similarly unified much of India, a pro-

cess continued several centuries later under the Hindu Gupta dynasty (A.D. 320–515), which was a period of stability and great learning in India. Other important events during this period included the advent of Christianity, which was founded on the teachings of Jesus Christ, who was crucified in Jerusalem in A.D. 33, and of Islam, which was founded on the teachings of the Prophet Muhammad, who died in Mecca, Saudi Arabia, in A.D. 632.

Up until the ninth century, and as the most powerful state in east Asia, China had been extremely influential on its neighboring territories in terms of language and culture. In the ninth century, this influence began to decline, and several new states began to emerge. In Cambodia, the Khmer empire developed (c. A.D. 802), and in Japan, the establishment of a new capital at Heian (Kyoto) saw the beginnings of a more distinctive Japanese culture that was less aligned with China.

Between 1200 and 1600, a wave of new empires swept across Asia. Genghis Khan of Mongolia led the brutal forces of the Mongol empire in conquering central Asia and China, while the Turkish and Islamic Ottoman empire reached its height under Sulayman the Magnificent (1520–1566). The Mogul empire also developed during this time (c. 1504) from its base in Kabul, Afghanistan, and gained control over most of India by about 1700. Although Islamic, the Moguls were tolerant of India's Hindu population, and a distinctive Indo-Muslim artistic culture emerged that is still evident in many of India's palaces and temples.

The Terracotta Army near Xi'an, China, was made to protect the spirit of China's first emperor, Qin Shi Huangdi (259–210 B.C.), after his death. Containing about eight thousand life-size warriors, the army was discovered in 1974 by villagers digging a well.

FACT FILE

Buddhism was formed as a religion following the teachings of Siddartha Gautama, who lived in northern India between 560 and 482 B.C.

Jakarta, Indonesia, was a major shipping and trading port for the colonies of the Dutch East Indies. During Dutch control (1619–1949), it was known as Batavia.

Hong Kong's famous ferries sail the waters between Kowloon Peninsula and Hong Kong Island. Hong Kong returned to Chinese administration in 1997 having been a British trading port since 1842.

COLONIAL ASIA

The period from 1600 to 1945 saw large parts of Asia come under the control of European maritime nations. The first contact with Europeans came through Portuguese spice traders, but other European nations—specifically the Spanish, Dutch, French, and British—soon sought their own share of this lucrative trade. Representatives of these countries established coastal ports to supply and transport Asian produce back to Europe. Several of these ports are now among Asia's biggest cities, including Kolkata, Karachi, Singapore, Hong Kong, Jakarta, and Shanghai. Over time, the European nations used their wealth and military superiority to impose colonial rule over large areas of the continent. During this period, the colonial powers extracted raw materials from their Asian colonies for export to Europe and then imported finished products back into the colonies. This practice undermined many local industries and consolidated national resources into the hands of a privileged few—a pattern that persists in many countries today.

FACT FILE

Between 1862 and 1943, the United States held a trading post named Hongkew in the Chinese city of Shanghai. The trading post was granted to the United States by the British, following their victory over China in a war over trading rights in 1842.

CENTURY OF TURMOIL

The twentieth century in Asia was marked by conflict and revolution. The early part of the century saw China emerge from almost two thouand years of dynastic rule when Sun Zhongshan (Sun Yatsen) formed a united China in 1911. Unification was short-lived, however, and from 1912, power struggles and civil war led to a fragmented China controlled by numerous warlords. The first half of the twentieth century saw Japan emerge as a major Asian power and conquer much of eastern China. The Japanese also conquered Korea and Taiwan, but further expansionist ambitions brought the Japanese empire into conflict with the United States and Britain, which had both previously supported Japan. On December 7, 1941, the Japanese attacked the U.S. naval base in Hawaii, pulling the United States into World War II. The United States eventually brought about the end of the war when it dropped two atomic bombs on the Japanese cities of Hiroshima and Nagasaki in August 1945.

The A-Bomb Dome in Hiroshima, Japan, was one of the few buildings left standing after the United States bombed the city in 1945. The shell of the building is now a permanent memorial to the tragedy and has become a symbol for peace.

World War II severely weakened Europe, and as a result, most Asian colonies were able to gain their independence in the years that followed. The Indian Subcontinent gained independence from Britain in 1947 and was split by a process known as "partition" to become three independent countries—Pakistan, India, and Bangladesh (East Pakistan until 1971). In 1947, another British colony, Palestine, was divided by the United Nations into an Arab state and a Jewish state. Arabs rejected the plan, however, and fighting broke out that led to the creation of the Jewish state of Israel in May 1948. Further fighting between Arab countries and Israel has continued ever since, with major wars over the control of lands in and around Israel erupting in 1956, 1967, and 1973. Disputes over land have still not been settled, and almost continuous tension and violence remain between Israel and the Palestinians (the Arab people who claim rights to the land).

COMMUNIST ASIA

After World War II, the Union of Soviet Socialist Republics (Soviet Union) emerged as a major superpower to rival the power of the United States. The two countries had very different beliefs. The United States believes in democracy and a free market economy, whereas the Soviet Union had followed a communist path of development since the Russian Revolution of 1917. Communism is a social and political ideology in which class systems are abolished and property and wealth are centrally owned and controlled by the community, for the community. In reality, Soviet communism led to the government's control of almost all aspects of life, such as where people lived, studied, and worked.

Many nations around the world aligned themselves behind one of these belief systems in what came to be known as the "Cold War." China became a Communist state in 1949 under Mao Zedong, and by the 1950s, communist ideas were spreading into Southeast Asia. Eager to repel the advance of communism there, the United States became heavily involved in the politics of the region. Nowhere was this more so than in Vietnam, where the United States fought a long and costly war (1964–1975) in a failed attempt to prevent Communist

U.S. soldiers from a 3rd Brigade, 25th Division task force enter a Vietnamese village in May 1967 during operations as part of the Vietnam War.

North Vietnam from capturing non-Communist South Vietnam. The Cold War ended in 1991, following the collapse and break-up of the Soviet Union. Many of Asia's newest states, such as Kazakhstan, Georgia, and Azerbaijan, emerged as a result of this breakup, and all of the former Soviet states are now adopting and adjusting to the ideas of democratic governance and a free market. China and North Korea are the last remaining Communist states in Asia.

A TURBULENT TURN

In 1990, a dispute over oil led Iraq to invade neighboring Kuwait and declare it a province of Iraq. The international community demanded Iraq's withdrawal. When Saddam Hussein, Iraq's dictator, refused, the United States led an international coalition and successfully ousted Iraq from Kuwait in the 1991 Gulf War. Hussein remained in power, however, and international sanctions failed to topple his Iraqi regime. It eventually fell following U.S.-led military action in 2003. In 1996, an armed group called the Taliban took control of Afghanistan (with support from Pakistan, Saudi Arabia, and the United States) after years of infighting between rival groups. Once in power, the Taliban introduced a strict and brutal Islamic regime that quickly attracted world criticism for its abuses of human rights. U.S.-led forces invaded Afghanistan and removed the Taliban from power in late 2001. After a period of rebuilding, democratic elections were held in October 2004 to elect a new Afghan government. Events in Iraq and Afghanistan mark a turbulent start to the century for Asia and have refocused the world's attention on the very area from which the world's first civilizations began.

Election officials count votes in Afghanistan's first democratic presidential elections. Hamid Karzai won 55 percent of the vote and was sworn into office as president in December 2004.

2. ASIAN ENVIRONMENTS

ALMOST EVERY ECOSYSTEM ON EARTH CAN BE FOUND IN ASIA, A FEAT unmatched by any other continent. Some Asian environments are virtually untouched by humans, such as the tundra of northern Russia. Others, including some river valleys, fertile plains, and forests, have suffered greatly under the pressures of Asia's enormous population.

The Tsho Rolpa glacier lake in the Himalayas is on the border between Nepal and China.

TOP OF THE WORLD

The Himalayas are the world's highest mountains with 110 peaks that are more than 23,950 feet (7,300 m) high. They straddle about 1,800 miles (2,900 km) along the border between India and Tibet (which is currently under Chinese control) and completely dominate the mountain kingdoms of Nepal and Bhutan. The Himalayas began forming about 40–50 million years ago when two tectonic plates met and began to crumple upward against each other. This uplift continues today, and the relatively young Himalayas (in geological terms) are still growing by as much as 0.4 inches (1 centimeter) per year.

PLATEAU OF LIFE

The Himalayas form the southern edge of the Tibetan Plateau— a vast area of mountains, gorges, and deserts. It is the largest and

highest plateau on Earth, covering an area of about 965,250 square miles (2.5 million sq km) and at an average elevation of more than 16,400 feet (5,000 m). The plateau itself is sparsely populated. It is of great significance to the livelihoods of billions of Asians, however, because it is the source for several of the continent's major rivers, including the Yangtze, Ganges, Indus, and Mekong rivers. The meltwater collected by these rivers are a lifeline for billions of people living downstream in Asia's plains and river valleys. Besides providing water, the rivers carry enormous volumes of nutrient-rich sediment from the plateau. The Yangtze, for instance, is thought to carry and deposit up to 551 million tons (500 million tonnes) of sediment per year. Some of Asia's best farmland is found in the valleys and plains where this sediment is deposited. They include the Gangetic plains of India and the Indus valley of Pakistan.

IN FOCUS: Fragile Earth

Much of Asia is affected by the continuing geological movements of Earth's tectonic plates. On December 26, 2004, a major earthquake in the Indian Ocean provided tragic evidence of just how vulnerable Asia and its people can be to such events. The quake triggered a massive tsunami wave that traveled at speeds of up to 500 miles (800 km) per hour over thousands of miles (kilometers), even reaching Africa. When it struck land, the force of the water smashed into villages and coastal resorts in Indonesia, Thailand, India, Sri Lanka, and numerous island chains, including the Maldives. An estimated 300,000 people were killed and millions left homeless. The United Nations believes it will take ten years for the areas affected to recover.

The city of Banda Aceh on Sumatra, Indonesia, was devastated by the December 2004 tsunami.

A man tills his small farm on the banks of the Mekong River in Khong Chiam, Thailand.

RIVERS OF WOE

The vast amounts of water carried by Asia's rivers can sometimes turn them from life-givers into life-takers. The Huang He, or Yellow River, in China is particularly prone to flooding and has killed more people than any other river in the world. The Huang He has a very high silt content of up to 70 percent by volume, and when swollen with abnormal amounts of water, the main river channel can not cope with the additional flow and bursts its banks. In 1931, the banks of the Huang He burst and caused the world's worst recorded flood. More than 4 million people were killed, and even more were left homeless.

The Yangtze, China's other major river, is also prone to flooding and last experienced serious flooding in 1998. The Chinese government has taken measures to reduce the risk of future floods. In the upper Yangtze region, millions of trees are being planted to absorb rainwater and reduce soil erosion, and in the floodplain, lakes are being restored that will allow floodwaters to disperse naturally rather than threaten settlements and farmland downstream.

INLAND SEAS

Western Asia is noted for its several inland seas. The Caspian Sea, shared by Azerbaijan, Russia, Kazakhstan, Turkmenistan, and Iran, is the largest inland water body in the world. It covers an area of 143,550 square miles (371,800 sq km), which is roughly the same size as Japan or the U.S. state of Montana.

••••••➤ IN FOCUS: The Aral Sea

The Aral Sea was once the fourth-largest lake in the world with an area of 24,904 square miles (64,501 sq km). In the 1960s, the former Soviet Union diverted water from the sea's tributaries, the Amu Darya and Syr Darya rivers, into irrigation projects for growing cotton in what is now Uzbekistan. The flow of water into the Aral Sea was dramatically reduced, and it had shrunk to less than half its size by 1995. Some former lakeshore communities found themselves living 62 miles (100 km) from the water. The Aral Sea is still shrinking today and is considered one of the world's worst ecological disasters.

Fishing boats lie abandoned on the former bed of the Aral Sea in Muynak, Uzbekistan.

The Aral Sea in Kazakhstan and Uzbekistan and the Dead Sea in Israel and Jordan are also inland seas. The Black Sea, which is shared by Turkey and five other countries, is almost an inland sea, but it has a connection to the Mediterranean via the Bosporus Strait. This narrow channel is considered a geographical division between Europe and Asia.

WHERE THERE IS NO WATER

The largest desert in Asia is the Arabian Desert in southern Saudi Arabia. Also known as *Rub' al Khali* (The Empty Quarter), it covers an area of 899,614 square miles

FACT FILE

Lake Baikal, near Russia's border with Mongolia, is the world's deepest lake at 5,371 feet (1,637 m). Its incredible depth means the lake contains an estimated 20 percent of Earth's fresh surface water—the same as all five of North America's Great Lakes combined.

The sand dunes of the Arabian Desert near Riyadh, Saudi Arabia, are a popular tourist attraction.

FACT FILE

Asia has about 140,000 miles (224,000 km) of coastline, much of it intensively settled with fishing communities. Asia produces and consumes more fish and other marine products, such as shellfish and seaweed, than any other continent.

(2,330,000 sq km) and is the largest continuous sand desert in the world. It is connected to another desert in northern Saudi Arabia called the Nafud, where giant sand dunes reach more than 328 feet (100 m) in height. Asia's other major deserts are the Gobi Desert in Mongolia and China, the Takla Makan Desert of northwestern China, and the Kara Kum Desert in Turkmenistan—all among the world's ten largest deserts. These desert environments have very little water, and daytime temperatures in the Arabian Desert can reach 129° Fahrenheit (54° Celsius). Consequently, Asia's deserts are largely unpopulated except near sources of water, such as rivers, oases, or where groundwater has been tapped.

DESERTIFICATION

Across Asia, large areas are at risk of desertification, a process in which soils take on desert-like characteristics, becoming unproductive and threatening livelihoods. Desertification is caused by mismanaged soil, normally due to overcultivation, overgrazing, or deforestation. The most severely affected countries include Pakistan, India, Iran, Mongolia, and China. In 2004, desertification was estimated to affect 27 percent of China, which is home to about 400 million people. China's deserts were growing at an average rate of 950 square miles (2,460 sq km) per year, and the economic impact of declining agricultural yields was estimated at US$6.5 billion a year. Along with more than twenty other Asian nations, China has formed a National Action Program (NAP) to combat the threat of desertification. In China, this effort has focused on planting trees in the areas most at risk of desertification. Up to 9.884 million acres (4 million hectares) of plantations are being created each year, and farmers are being paid to plant their land with trees instead of farming it.

FORESTS AND TUNDRA

Asian Russia is considered to be everything east of the Ural Mountains. This area is frequently referred to as Siberia and accounts for about 75 percent of Russia's total land area but only 20 percent of its population. Northern Siberia is made up mainly of arctic tundra, a bitterly cold environment with temperatures well below freezing for most of the year. The ground has a permanent layer of frozen soils (permafrost) that reach depths of more than 4,900 feet (1,500 m). South of the tundra is a habitat known as taiga. It is a marshy region of coniferous forests of fir, pine, larch, and cedar trees that covers about 60 percent of Russia. It is the largest forest in the

Sands from the Gobi Desert engulf Beijing, China, in a dust storm during April 2000. The desert expanded by 20,240 square miles (52,400 sq km) between 1994 and 1999 and is now within 150 miles (240 km) of Beijing.

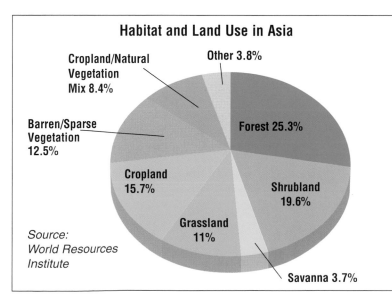

Habitat and Land Use in Asia

Cropland/Natural Vegetation Mix 8.4%

Other 3.8%

Barren/Sparse Vegetation 12.5%

Forest 25.3%

Cropland 15.7%

Shrubland 19.6%

Grassland 11%

Source: World Resources Institute

Savanna 3.7%

Tundra dominates much of Siberia in eastern Russia, such as here in the Magadan region.

world—three times the size of the Amazon rain forest.

Forests are also a significant feature of Southeast Asia. Indonesia, Malaysia, Thailand, Cambodia, Laos, and Vietnam all have significant areas of tropical rain forest. Indonesia's rain forests are particularly important because they are the habitat of a large number of species and make up about 10 percent of the world's remaining rain forests.

THE ASIAN MONSOON

Asia's climate varies from arctic conditions in the north to a tropical climate in the southeast. The range of climates is so complex that it is impossible to generalize, but an important climatic feature for much of Asia is the monsoon. The monsoon is a seasonal shift in wind patterns caused by the north-south movement of the Sun and changes in the temperature of the Asian landmass. The summer monsoon occurs as the northerly movement of the Sun heats the landmass, forcing hot air upward and creating a pocket of low pressure. This condition draws in warm moist air from the Indian Ocean, heavily laden with rain. The monsoon and its rains are not entirely predictable but

Women weed rice paddies in the southern Indian state of Kerala. Like many Asian farmers, the success of their harvest is dependent on the rains of the Asian monsoon.

normally reach Sri Lanka in early May and move northward to reach northern India by mid-July, with its arrival signaling the planting season for millions of farmers. During the northern winter monsoon, the cooling of northern and central Asia creates high pressure and reverses the air currents, driving cool dry winds southward. The winter monsoon begins in northern India about September and reaches India's southern tip about mid-November.

FACT FILE

Almost one-quarter of the world's population depends on the Asian monsoon and its life-giving summer rains for their livelihoods.

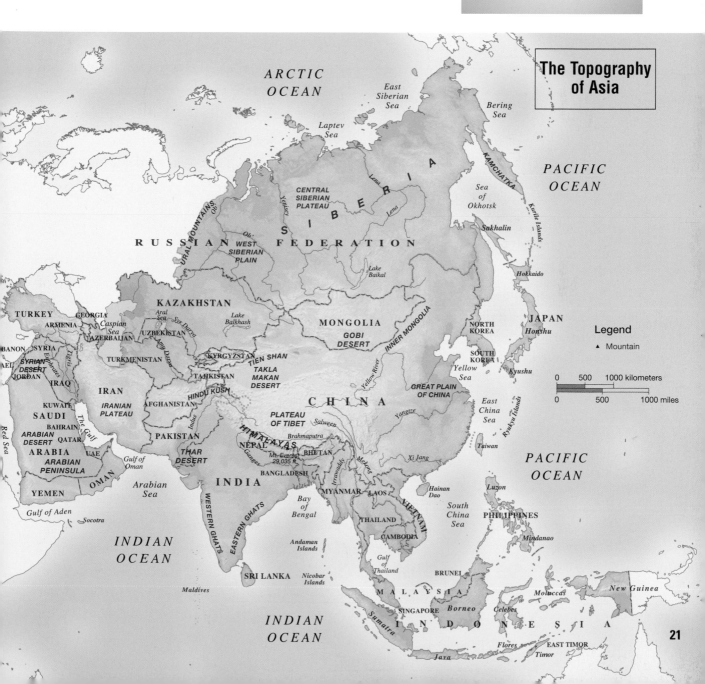

The Topography of Asia

Legend

▲ Mountain

0   500   1000 kilometers

0   500   1000 miles

3. THE PEOPLE OF ASIA

*T*HE COMPOSITION AND WELL-BEING OF ASIA'S POPULATION IS INCREDIBLY varied. It possesses the largest ethnic group in the world, the Han Chinese —who number almost 1.2 billion people—but is also home to several of the world's smallest groups. The Jarawa of India's Andaman Islands are thought to number fewer than 300 people. In terms of well-being, the Japanese have the world's highest life expectancy of 81.5 years, compared with just 43 years in Afghanistan. Only 13 percent of Afghanistan's population has access to safe drinking water, while in Japan it is universally available. Similar contrasts can be found throughout Asia's vast population, which accounts for almost 2 in 3 of the world's people.

A Pwo Karen woman carries clean water home from the village well near Omkoi in the Chiang Mai area of Northern Thailand.

FACT FILE

The Han Chinese are an ethnic group that makes up about 92 percent of China's population. They number more than the combined population of Europe and the United States.

GROWING NUMBERS

Asia's population grew rapidly during the second half of the last century from about 1.4 billion in 1950 to about 4 billion by 2005, an increase greater than the entire world population in 1950. Such rapid population growth is explained by dramatic improvements in medicine and in people's standards of living, leading to higher life expectancies and reduced infant mortality. In China, life expectancy at birth has increased from 36 years in 1960 to 71 years today, while in Iran infant mortality has fallen from 164 per thousand live births in 1960 to fewer than 34. As more children survive and adults live longer, the population begins to grow. In addition to these natural changes, large families are considered valuable in many parts of Asia for economic or cultural reasons. A large family means more available labor for working in the fields, the factory, or around the home. Children also provide a form of social security in places where there is no government system, because they will help to provide and care for their aging parents. Some cultures also consider large families a sign of status, so parents may choose to have large families even when many children are unnecessary.

A young girl being immunized in Tehran, Iran. Immunization programs have dramatically improved child survival rates in Iran and other Asian countries.

Asia has a youthful population with about 36 percent of the population, or 1.4 billion people, below the age of 18. When Asia's young start their own families, the population will continue growing due to a process called population momentum. By 2050, Asia is expected to reach a population of about 5.2 billion. Only a handful of Asia's more developed nations, such as Japan, South Korea, and the countries of the former Soviet Union, will see a decline in their population. This decline will result from lower birth rates and an aging of the population in these countries.

FACT FILE

At current growth rates, India will surpass China as the world's most populous nation in about 2045. By 2050, India will be home to more than 1.5 billion people.

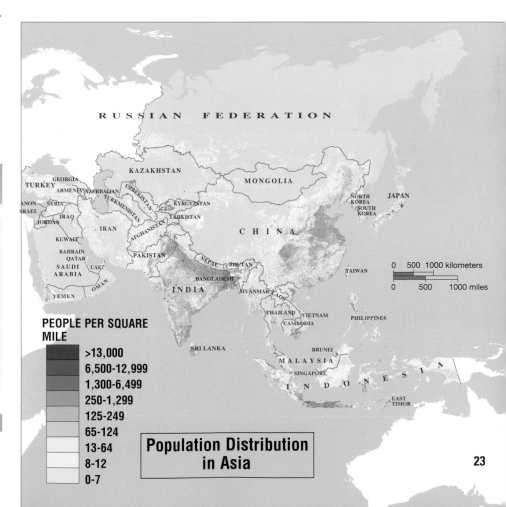

Population Distribution in Asia

PEOPLE PER SQUARE MILE

- >13,000
- 6,500-12,999
- 1,300-6,499
- 250-1,299
- 125-249
- 65-124
- 13-64
- 8-12
- 0-7

23

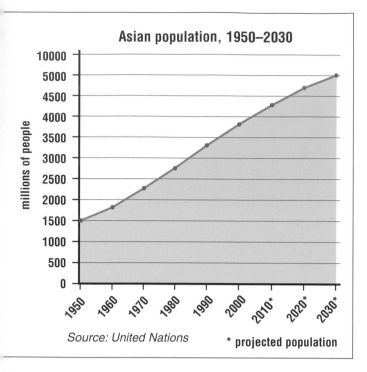

Asian population, 1950–2030

millions of people

(y-axis values: 0, 500, 1000, 1500, 2000, 2500, 3000, 3500, 4000, 4500, 5000, 10000)

(x-axis values: 1950, 1960, 1970, 1980, 1990, 2000, 2010*, 2020*, 2030*)

Source: United Nations   * projected population

Villagers in Orissa state, India, watch a health education and family planning video from the back of a mobile health unit.

FORCE OR CHOICE?

Rapid population growth places extreme pressure on governments to provide health, education, and other services. India's population grew by more than 170 million in the 1990s alone. In 1976, the Indian government, under Prime Minister Indira Ghandi, took drastic action to reduce population growth by introducing a policy of forced sterilization of the poor. The policy proved extremely unpopular and is widely blamed for the government's defeat in elections the following year. Several Indian states still offer financial incentives for people to be sterilized, but they are no longer forced to do so.

Today, most governments focus on helping parents make their own choices about the size of their families. This "family planning" approach focuses on providing information and, sometimes, distributing free or subsidized contraceptives. When given this kind of support, many parents voluntarily limit their family size. One difficulty in many Asian countries is that women do not enjoy the same rights as men and may not be given access to family planning services, particularly in countries dominated by strict Islamic beliefs where men dominate decision making. As a result, population growth in the countries of Yemen, Oman, Kuwait, Saudi Arabia, and others remains very high at up to 3.6 percent a year. This rate compares to an Asian average of 1.3 percent and a world average of 1.2 percent a year. Population experts agree that for population growth to slow across Asia, women must be given equal rights and empowered to make their own decisions about the number of children they have.

URBANIZATION

After Africa, Asia is the world's least urbanized continent with 39 percent of the population living in urban centers in 2003. In several countries, however, urbanization is

FACT FILE

China's one child policy is estimated to have prevented about 250 million births between 1980 and 2000. This number is almost the same as the total U.S. population.

●●●●●●● ▶ IN FOCUS: China's one child policy

In 1979, China introduced a policy limiting married couples to a single child. The only three exceptions made are for ethnic minority groups, when a first child is born with a disability, or when both parents are single children themselves. For other parents, having a second child would result in a fine and could cost them their jobs or housing. In addition, the second child would be unregistered and, therefore, unable to attend school or receive health care. As a result of this policy, many pregnancies are terminated, sometimes under great pressure from population officials. A cultural preference for boys—because they traditionally support aging parents—has meant that more girls are aborted than boys. Some baby girls are even left to die so that parents may try again for a boy. These trends have resulted in an extremely unbalanced population. In 2000, figures suggested that 117 boys were born for every 100 girls and that this ratio could be as high as 131 to 100. A fierce debate continues about whether China's one child policy is a success story or a breach of basic human rights. The long-term impact for future population patterns are also unknown, but one likely outcome is that Chinese men who wish to marry will increasingly have to look for foreign brides due to a shortage of Chinese women.

A woman and her single child visit a local market. China's single child policy is almost three decades old.

New high-rise apartment blocks spring up around the outskirts of Hong Kong—one of the most densely populated and heavily urbanized regions in the world.

substantially higher at 90–100 percent in Singapore, Hong Kong, Israel, Qatar, Bahrain, and Kuwait. In contrast, less than 20 percent of the people in Cambodia, Bhutan, and Nepal live in urban centers. In the Asian countries with the three largest populations—China, India, and Indonesia—the urbanization rates are 39, 28, and 46 percent respectively.

Despite relatively low rates of urbanization, Asia is home to several of the world's largest cities. Tokyo, the most populous city in the world, had 35 million people in 2003. Any city with more than 10 million people is known as a megacity, and Asia had eleven of the world's twenty megacities in 2003. In addition to Tokyo, they are Mumbai, Delhi, and Kolkata, India; Shanghai and Beijing, China; Dhaka, Bangladesh; Jakarta, Indonesia; Osaka-Kobe, Japan; Karachi, Pakistan; and Manila in the Philippines. Istanbul, Turkey, is expected to join the list soon as Asia's twelfth megacity.

URBAN STANDARDS

Urban growth has been extremely rapid across much of Asia. Dhaka's population, for instance,

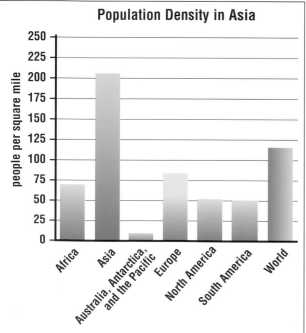

Population Density in Asia

people per square mile

Source: United Nations; Britannica Book of the Year 2004

FACT FILE

Asia has the highest population density in the world at almost 214 people per square mile (83 per sq km). Singapore and Hong Kong have almost 16,000 per square mile (6,200 per sq km), while Macau has an incredible 43,010 people per square mile (16,530 per sq km)!

An urban waterway clogged with refuse and sewage in Mumbai, India. Pollution like this is a serious health hazard to residents.

grew by more than 6 percent per year between 1975 and 2000, equivalent to adding 875 people every day. Few cities can keep pace with this level of growth, and living conditions are often poor as a result. Jakarta, Indonesia, has a population of about 12.5 million people but with no sewerage system. About 73 percent of Jakarta's households have septic tanks, but these pollute local water supplies and frequently overflow onto city streets. People without septic tanks simply defecate in the streets or into plastic bags that are then thrown into local ditches or rivers—known as "wrap and throw" sanitation. With similar conditions in other Indonesian cities, illnesses such as gastroenteritis and typhoid are common. The cost of lost work time and treatment for these illnesses has been estimated at more than US$4.7 billion a year.

FACT FILE

Asia includes seven of the ten most populous countries in the world—China, India, Indonesia, Pakistan, Russia, Bangladesh, and Japan.

●●●●●▶IN FOCUS: The Orangi Pilot Project

Many Asian cities share Jakarta's sanitation problems, but some, such as the Orangi district of Karachi, Pakistan, have developed solutions. Home to about 1.2 million people, the district began a self-help program in 1980 called the Orangi Pilot Project (OPP) to improve sanitation. The community formed neighborhood teams (according to the streets within the settlement) and combined their labor and finances toward the installation of a basic sewage system. Each street built and maintained its own system using locally supplied materials, and these were gradually connected to form a district system. More than ninety thousand households are now connected to the system, which was built for just US$30 per household. The success of the OPP is now being copied in other Pakistani cities, as well as elsewhere in Asia.

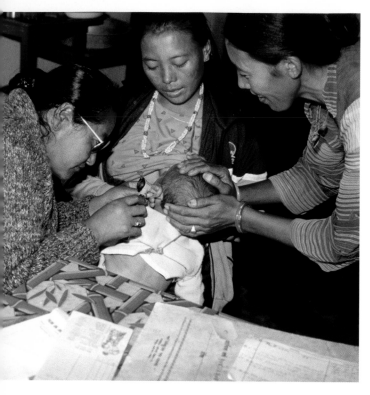

HEALTH CARE

Countries such as Japan, South Korea, Singapore, Israel, and much of the Middle East have health care comparable to that in Europe or North America. Across the rest of Asia, the availability of health care varies considerably. In Kazakhstan, for example, there are about 260 people per doctor, whereas in Thailand this ratio increases to 3,333 people per doctor, and to more than 16,660 in Bhutan and Nepal.

Across large parts of Asia, basic health needs, such as clean water and sanitation, are woefully inadequate. In China, Indonesia, and Vietnam, about one-quarter of the population lacks access to safe water. In Oman, Laos, and Cambodia, this number increases to more than 60 percent of the population. Shortages of these basic needs are significant because the majority of diseases in Asia (typhoid, diarrhea, hepatitis A, and cholera) are related to poor quality water and sanitation.

Health care facilities are stretched very thinly in countries like Nepal. Western-trained nurses examine this child in Pokhara, Nepal. Many Asian countries, including Nepal, have a shortage of trained medical staff.

MAJOR DISEASES

Malaria is a disease carried by mosquitoes and found across large parts of Asia, from Afghanistan through Pakistan, India, and into Southeast Asia as far as southern Indonesia. Southern China and Yemen, in the Arab peninsula, are also affected. Although preventable and treatable with antimalarial drugs, malaria parasites are now resistant to drugs in many countries. In addition, the drugs are too expensive for many poorer communities to acquire.

HIV infection rates are increasing rapidly in Asia, and many experts believe that Asia could soon replace Africa as the center of the global HIV epidemic. There are already up to 11 million people living with HIV/AIDS across Asia, and more than one million new people were infected in 2003 alone. Southeast Asia is the region with the highest infection levels, while the fewest are in the Middle East and East Asia. Poorer communities are most affected because they are generally less educated and less aware of the ways in which HIV is transmitted.

AN EDUCATED CONTINENT

Education is highly valued across Asia and has helped the continent to develop a highly skilled and able workforce. Companies and governments in other parts of the world, such as Europe, Australia, and North America, actively recruit Asian graduates to fill skill gaps within their own labor force. This practice is especially true in the medical, engineering, and computer fields. Not all Asians, however, benefit from an education. Less than three-quarters of children in southern Asia attend primary school, and one-third of these will fail to complete their basic education (five primary years). Poverty is normally the cause for these drop outs, but in agricultural societies parents may choose to keep their children from school in order to have help in the fields or around the home. In Muslim communities, girls may be denied the opportunity to go to school at all. Under Afghanistan's Taliban regime (1995–2001), girls were banned from school, and those being educated in secrecy risked severe punishment. Even in the more moderate Muslim societies of the Middle East, girls frequently have fewer opportunities than boys to complete their schooling.

A counselor delivers an HIV education seminar to community members in a district of Jakarta, Indonesia's capital. HIV/AIDS is relatively new to Indonesia but is spreading quickly.

4. ASIAN CULTURE AND RELIGION

DAILY LIFE IN ASIA IS STRONGLY INFLUENCED BY PEOPLE'S RELIGIOUS beliefs and festivals, and religious events are celebrated by millions in some of the biggest gatherings of humanity on the planet. Islam, Christianity, Hinduism, Judaism, Buddhism, and Sikhism are major global religions that all have their origins in Asia. In Eastern Asia, more localized belief systems can be found, including Shinto from Japan and Confucianism and Taoism from China.

PRIMARY RELIGION

Most Asian countries are dominated by a single religion. Saudi Arabia, Iran, Iraq, Pakistan, Afghanistan, Turkey, and Azerbaijan are all more than 90 percent Islamic. Buddhism is the majority religion in Cambodia, Thailand, Bhutan, Burma, and Laos, whereas in India and Nepal, Hinduism is the most common. Christianity dominates in the Philippines and Judaism in Israel. China is unusual because it is officially an "atheist state"—having no sanctioned religion. Buddhism and Christianity are both practiced in China, however, and the government has become more tolerant of these religious faiths in recent years. In fact, China is said to have one of the world's fastest growing Christian populations.

The dragon dance, here being performed in Beijing, China's capital, is a traditional part of Chinese New Year celebrations. The spread of Chinese culture means that Chinese New Year is now celebrated in many western nations, too.

RELIGION AND CONFLICT

The majority of Asians live peacefully alongside each other, with their differing beliefs irrelevant. In some parts of the continent, however, people with different belief systems clash over issues, such as political control or over competing rights to disputed territory. Kashmir has been an area of dispute since 1947, when India gained independence from Britain and was partitioned into India (mainly Hindu) and Pakistan (mainly Islamic). Kashmir lies right on the border of this divide. It is part of the northern Indian state of Jammu and Kashmir—the only Indian state to have a mainly Islamic population. Pakistan has long claimed that, because of this, Jammu and Kashmir should be part of Muslim Pakistan. India, however has claimed sovereignty over Jammu and Kashmir since it was ceded to India in October 1947. Thousands have died in the ongoing conflict over this state.

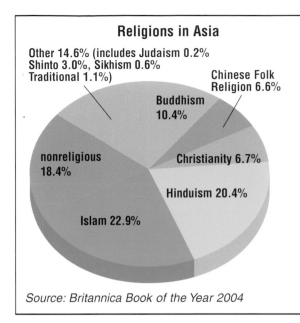

Religions in Asia

Other 14.6% (includes Judaism 0.2% Shinto 3.0%, Sikhism 0.6% Traditional 1.1%)

Chinese Folk Religion 6.6%

Buddhism 10.4%

Christianity 6.7%

nonreligious 18.4%

Hinduism 20.4%

Islam 22.9%

Source: Britannica Book of the Year 2004

SACRED CITY

The city of Jerusalem in Israel is a spiritual center for three world religions—Christianity, Islam, and Judaism. Every year, millions of people travel to the city to visit its numerous religious sites. These sacred places include the Western "Wailing" Wall (the holiest Jewish site), the Church of the Holy Sepulchre (Christianity's holiest site, where Jesus is said to have been crucified), and the Dome of the Rock (from where it is believed Muhammad, the founder of Islam, ascended to Heaven). With its shared religious claims, Jerusalem is one of the most contested pieces of land in the world and lies at the heart of tensions within the Middle East.

The Dome of the Rock in Jerusalem, Israel, is the oldest surviving structure in the Islamic world, dating back to A.D. 691. It is built on Haram esh-Sharif (Temple Mount), which is sacred to both Muslims and Jews.

PILGRIMS AND FESTIVALS

Asia is witness to some of the world's greatest pilgrimages and several of the largest festivals ever known. One of the greatest spectacles on Earth is the annual Hajj that takes place in Mecca, Saudi Arabia. It is the ultimate pilgrimage for all Muslims, and one that every Muslim will try to make at least once in his or her life. Up to 2 million people gather in Mecca each year to perform a series of rituals that together comprise the Hajj.

FAMILY VALUES

The family is an important institution in Asia. Families gather to celebrate festivals, such as the Hindu celebration Diwali or the Chinese New Year. Marriages are also important events. In India, they can attract thousands of guests from enormous extended families. In Asia, families are also an important form of economic support. Children

●●●●●●● ▶ IN FOCUS: Maha Kumbh Mela

Hindus celebrate many different festivals, but nothing compares to the *Maha Kumbh Mela* (Great Pitcher Festival). It takes place every three years and rotates between four locations in India. The Maha Kumbh Mela at Allahabad, where the Ganges, Yamuna, and mythical Saraswati rivers meet, is considered the most sacred location. In 2001, more than 110 million pilgrims came to bathe in the waters and perform a ritual washing away of their sins.

Pilgrims and *sadhus* (holy men) gather for the 2001 Maha Kumbh Mela at Allahabad.

have traditionally cared for their elders, and wealthy relatives are expected to assist those who are less fortunate. These close family ties extend into the business world, and many of Asia's most successful companies are built around a single family. The *chaebols* of South Korea are a good example of these ties. Chaebols are large groups of companies that are normally controlled by a single family. The biggest chaebols have become world-known brands and include Hyundai, Samsung, LG, and Daewoo.

A GLOBAL INFLUENCE

Some aspects of Asian culture have a global influence. The popularity of Asian cuisine is one example, with Chinese, Thai, Indian, and Japanese dishes enjoyed worldwide. Martial arts, such as tae kwon do (Korea), kung fu (China), and judo and karate (Japan), have emerged from Asia to become major world sports. Asian philosophies have also spread widely, including feng-shui from China and yoga from India. Artistically, Asian designs and color patterns are used around the world, influencing architecture, clothing, furniture, and interior design, and even gardening.

The Hyundai shipyard in Ulsan, South Korea, is the largest in the world. It is owned by Hyundai, a family-run company known as a chaebol.

Yoshihiro Akiyama of Japan (*in blue*) throws Nyamkhuu Damdinsuren of Mongolia to win a match during the September 2003 World Judo Championships held in Osaka, Japan.

FACT FILE

Indian food is the most popular cuisine for dining out and takeout in the United Kingdom. London has more Indian restaurants than the Indian cities of Mumbai, Kolkata, Dehli, and Madras combined!

A craftsman carves a Garuda sculpture in Bali, Indonesia—well known for its wood carving.

Elaborate costumes and makeup add to the drama of kathakali dancing in southern India.

SKILLED ARTISANS

Asia's artisans are remarkably skilled and produce a wide range of goods. Indonesia is well known for woodcarving and batik, China for pottery and painting, India for hand-printed textiles and jewelry, and Iran for its Persian carpets and rugs. Several art forms are uniquely Asian, including calligraphy, a form of writing that originated in China, and origami, artistic paper folding that originated in Japan. Japan has also made popular the Chinese art of growing miniature trees, known as *bonsai*.

PERFORMING ARTS

India's movie industry is arguably the most famous of Asia's performing arts today, and India produces more films than any other country. The industry is centered in Mumbai (formerly called Bombay) and has become known as "Bollywood." Nearly all the films include music and dancing and are normally centered around a love story and a main hero or heroine. The movies' elaborate sets and beautiful costumes are a link to more traditional performing arts in India. One of these is kathakali dancing from Kerala in southern India. Kathakali dancers are famous for their colorful three-dimensional makeup and costumes. The dancers tell traditional stories by performing a combination of dance and mime. The movement of their eyes, the whites of which are dyed red for the performance, plays a particular role in expressing the emotions of the stories.

SPORTS IN ASIA

Sports are popular across most of Asia, and a wide variety of sports are played. They include sports played around the world, such as soccer, cricket, and basketball, but others are unique to Asia, such as sumo wrestling in Japan or camel racing in the Middle East. Asia has produced many of the world's leading athletes in sports as varied as gymnastics, badminton, archery, and weightlifting.

At the 2004 Olympic Games in Athens, Greece, South Korea confirmed itself as the world's leading archery nation. Sung Hyun Park won the individual gold medal in women's archery and, together with her teammates, also won gold in the team event. South Korea also took gold in men's team archery. Badminton was completely dominated by Asian nations, with South Korea winning the men's doubles, Indonesia's Taufik Hidayat winning men's singles, and China claiming the women's and mixed medals.

South Korea's Im Dong Hyun takes aims during the men's archery competition at the Athens 2004 Olympic Games. He went on to help South Korea win the gold medal for the men's team event.

Watching sports in Asia is almost as important as participating in them, with sporting events attracting huge audiences. When India's cricket team is playing, city streets grind to a halt as everyone follows the fortunes of the team. South Koreans are similarly committed to their national soccer team, and national celebrations took place when the team reached the semi-finals of the 2002 World Cup, which South Korea hosted jointly with Japan. In August 2008, the attention of the sports world will be focused on Beijing, when China becomes the third Asian nation, after Japan (1964) and South Korea (1988), to host the Olympic Games.

5. NATURAL RESOURCES IN ASIA

*A*SIA IS RICH IN NATURAL RESOURCES AND PLAYS A PARTICULARLY KEY role in global energy supplies. For this reason, it has become a region of intense international attention. Some critics in the United States, the United Kingdom (U.K.), and abroad have accused both the United States and Britain of intervening in the Middle East, not for peace and stability as they claim, but to gain access to the region's oil.

Oil derricks and rigs fill the landscape around the Caspian Sea in Azerbaijan, a country rich in oil. The oil is extracted from both offshore and onshore operations.

OIL WEALTH

At the end of 2003, Asia (including the Russian Federation) accounted for 75 percent of the world's proven oil reserves and about 52 percent of its production. This immense oil wealth is overwhelmingly centered in the countries of the Middle East, with Saudi Arabia, Iran, Iraq, Kuwait, and United Arab Emirates (UAE) having the most significant reserves. Among other Asian nations, the oil reserves of the Caspian Sea region are thought to be the most significant. To date, these have been underutilized because of political disputes over who owns the reserves and practical difficulties

of how to export the oil from the region. Azerbaijan and Kazakhstan are leading the growth in the oil industry around the Caspian Sea, however, and they have increased their oil production by 70 percent since 1992. New pipelines have been built connecting the oil fields of the Caspian Sea to oil terminals on the Black Sea and Mediterranean

Sea. From there, oil is then transported by tanker to key oil markets in North America, Europe, and Eastern Asia, particularly Japan.

NATURAL GAS

Asia also contains substantial gas reserves, with 78 percent of proven reserves and 47 percent of global production at the end of 2003. The Russian Federation is the region's main source of

natural gas, with 27 percent of world reserves and 22 percent of global production. Other significant sources include Iran, Qatar, Saudi Arabia, and UAE, but they are also found in Bangladesh, Myanmar, Malaysia, and Vietnam, among others. Bangladesh's gas reserves are its only significant source of energy and are, therefore, of vital importance to its economy. Controversy exists over the potential export of Bangladeshi gas to neighboring countries, such as India, because Bangladeshis believe it should be used to benefit Bangladesh directly and not sold to earn foreign exchange. Plans include using natural gas as fuel for motor vehicles and to generate electricity. It can also be used to make agricultural fertilizers that are in high demand in Bangladesh.

Pipelines carry natural gas from the gas fields to the refinery in the Yamburg area of Russia. Natural gas exported from Russia is key to meeting European energy needs.

COAL

Asia contains about 41 percent of the world's known coal reserves, with the majority of these located in the Russian Federation, China, and India. More than half of the world's coal (51 percent) is produced in Asian countries, with China alone accounting for 33.5 percent of global output. Much of China's coal is used to fuel its rapidly expanding industrial economy, but this dependence on coal has had serious environmental implications because China's coal is mainly "brown coal," which is particularly high in sulphur and releases large quantities of sulphur dioxide as it is burned. When sulphur dioxide is mixed with water vapor in the atmosphere, it forms acid rain, which damages plants and buildings and contaminates water sources when it falls to Earth. Large volumes of carbon dioxide, one of the main gases associated with global warming, are also released. China produces about 12 percent of the world's carbon emissions, second only to the United States' total of 24 percent.

HYDROELECTRIC POWER

Asia's rivers provide several countries with a resource that can be used to generate electricity. Known as hydroelectric power (HEP), this process works by channeling water through turbines that generate electricity as the force of falling water causes them to turn. Bhutan, Nepal, Laos, Kyrgyzstan, and

An open pit coal mine creates a giant scar on the landscape of the city of Manzhouli, in Inner Mongolia, China. The country's rapid industrialization of recent years has relied heavily on its coal reserves for energy.

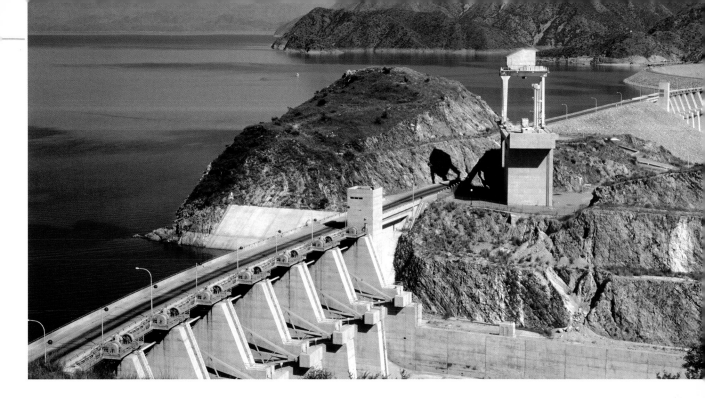

Tajikistan depend on HEP for more than 90 percent of their electricity supplies. Other Asian nations with significant HEP dependency include North Korea, Vietnam, Afghanistan, Japan, India, and China. India and China have both pursued large-scale dam building projects in recent years to harness their rivers for HEP. Several of these projects have caused controversy because of the potential social and environmental impact. The Three Gorges HEP project on China's Yangtze river, for example, will displace about 2 million people and submerge an estimated 1,650 settlements when it is completed in 2009. Environmental experts are also concerned that pollutants released during the flooding of industrial facilities could seriously contaminate the river.

Tarbela HEP Dam on the Indus River in Pakistan rises 485 feet (148 m) high and is 1.7 miles (2.7 km) long. Completed in 1977, the embankment contains 4.5 billion cubic feet (126 million cubic meters) of earth and rock, the largest volume ever used in a structure of its kind.

MINERALS

Asian nations produce a wide range of the world's key nonfuel minerals, including iron ore, bauxite, tin, chromium, titanium, fluorspar, and copper. Several countries have a lead role in the global supply of minerals. In 2002, China produced about 54 percent of the world's fluorspar—a raw material for making plastics and optical products—and 21 percent of its iron ore,

Wood is carried home by a young boy in Pakistan. The use of wood for cooking and heating in many Asian countries places the region's forests under increasing pressure.

FACT FILE

Between 1990 and 2000, Indonesia's forests were shrinking at a rate of about 3.2 million acres (1.3 million ha) each year. Wildlife, such as the already endangered orangutan, is severely threatened by this level of deforestation.

which is used to make steel. Kazakhstan accounted for 18 percent of the world's chromium (used to strengthen steel) and Indonesia for 9 percent of its copper.

FORESTS

Much of Asia's original forest cover has been cleared to make way for agricultural land or for settlements. Forest area has also declined due to the logging of trees for fuelwood, construction materials, or general timber. Wood is still important as an energy source, mainly for cooking, in several Asian countries, including India and China. In India, fuelwood was used by about 21 percent of urban households and 62 percent of rural households to meet their cooking needs in 2000.

The tropical forests of Southeast Asia are renowned for their high-quality tropical timbers. In 2002, Malaysia was the world's biggest exporter of tropical logs, and Malaysia and Indonesia were the leading exporters of tropical sawnwood and tropical plywood. The main markets for tropical timber from Southeast Asia are Japan, China, the United States, and Europe. In addition to logging in areas approved by Asian governments, there is a considerable volume of illegal logging in Southeast Asia. Indonesia is especially affected, and some experts believe that the illegal logging of Indonesia's forests equals, and maybe even exceeds, legal logging. The Indonesian government is trying to stop illegal logging through export bans (introduced in 2001) and increased policing of forests, but these measures have had minimal impact to date.

FISHERIES

Asia is the world's leading producer of fish, with China alone accounting for about 18 percent of the world catch. Japan, Indonesia, the Russian Federation, India, Thailand, and the Philippines are also key fishing nations, but fishing is important across much of the continent. It provides the main source of protein in the diets of millions of Asians and is also a major employer, with about 30 million fishermen employed across the continent. Asia's fisheries are considered a vital resource for meeting the food needs of its growing population, but some concern exists that fishing waters could become depleted if they are not carefully managed.

FACT FILE

China, Japan, Indonesia, the Russian Federation, India, Thailand, and the Philippines accounted for about 41 percent of the global fish catch in 2000.

The Jugalchi fish market in Pusan, South Korea, is one of the largest in Asia. Fisheries are an important element of the Asian economy.

• • • • ▶ IN FOCUS: Aquaculture

China is at the forefront of a revolution in fishing known as aquaculture, in which fish are farmed in ponds to produce food for human and/or animal consumption. Between 1970 and 2000, aquaculture's contribution to total global fish production increased from 3.9 percent to 27.3 percent. Asia is responsible for about 90 percent of current world aquaculture production and is also the area of fastest growth. One unique form of aquaculture found in China and Cambodia is the practice of farming fish alongside rice, the region's staple crop. The fish are raised in the flooded rice paddies, a farming system that has proven to be highly productive because the fish also help fertilize the rice.

6. THE ASIAN ECONOMY

ASIA IS SECOND ONLY TO AFRICA AS THE POOREST REGION OF the world and includes several of its poorest countries, such as Bangladesh, Cambodia, Nepal, Tajikistan, Nepal, and Laos. In Japan, however, Asia also has the world's second largest economy (after the United States). Several of the world's wealthiest nations, including Hong Kong, Singapore, and Kuwait, are also in Asia.

FACT FILE

More than two-thirds of the workforce, in China, Laos, Thailand, Vietnam, and Nepal, are employed in agriculture .

A woman works in a cornfield in northern Pakistan.

A MIXED ECONOMY

Traditionally agricultural, Asia's economic structure changed dramatically during the second half of the twentieth century, and Asia is today a truly mixed economy. Its industries include many of the world's leading manufacturers, and it is also home to an increasing proportion of the world's service industries. In 2000, the economic contributions for the continent as a whole by business sector were about 8 percent for agriculture, 35 percent for industry, and 57 percent for services. These averages, however, hide the continued importance of agriculture in several Asian economies. In Iran, for instance, agriculture still made up about 21 percent of the total economy in 2000, while in China, Pakistan, and India the figures were about 18, 24, and 28 percent, respectively. Agriculture is also important to Israel and Turkey, both of which have developed high-value agricultural exports of fruits and vegetables to nearby European markets.

INDUSTRIAL GROWTH

Asia's industrial growth came after World War II and was led by Japan, which focused on high- tech industrial production in its post-war rebuilding. Relatively poor in natural resources of its own, Japan's industries looked to its Asian neighbors for supplies of raw materials, which they converted into finished products for export to the more developed economies of Europe and North America. By the 1970s, Japan had become a major world economy and one of the leading producers of cars, steel, ships, electrical products, and other manufactured items.

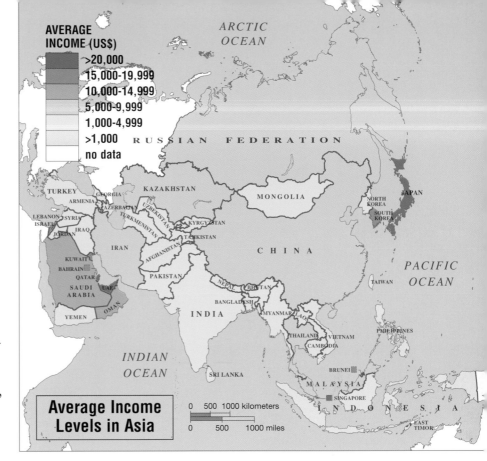

AVERAGE INCOME (US$)
- >20,000
- 15,000-19,999
- 10,000-14,999
- 5,000-9,999
- 1,000-4,999
- >1,000
- no data

Average Income Levels in Asia

0   500   1000 kilometers
0   500   1000 miles

Japan's success has been built around a business system called *Soga-Shosha* that develops enormous corporate conglomerates in which a family of individual businesses combine their resources. In such a system, trade takes place as much within the conglomerate as it does with external customers and suppliers. A Japanese company might, for example, buy the rights to mine iron ore in Indonesia and sell the ore to its steel plant in Japan. The steel that's produced may then be sold to Japanese automobile factories in Europe to make cars that are sold to Japanese car retailers in the United States. By controlling the chain of production and trade, Japanese businesses have amassed great wealth. South Korea is one of several Asian, and indeed global, countries to adopt elements of the Soga-Shosha business

Japan and South Korea have built a reputation for producing high-quality electronic goods, such as computers, mobile phones, and cameras.

The Petronas Towers in Kuala Lumpur, Malaysia, were the tallest buildings in the world until overtaken in 2004 by the Taipei 101 building in Taiwan. The Petronas Towers were completed just as the Asian economic crisis struck, and they remain half empty as the economy can not support full occupancy.

system. Known as *chaebols* in South Korea, these kinds of systems have been equally influential in the growth of South Korea's economy.

TIGERS IN CRISIS

Between the 1960s and mid-1990s, four Asian economies—Taiwan, Singapore, Hong Kong, and South Korea—achieved incredible economic growth by focusing on export industries and protecting their domestic markets from imported foreign goods. They became known as the "Asian Tigers" and were soon joined by Thailand, Malaysia, Indonesia, and the Philippines. These economies depended on foreign markets for their success but, in the mid 1990s, changes in global currency markets began to make their goods more expensive. Exports fell dramatically, and imports increased as exchange rates made imported goods less expensive.

In 1997, Thailand was forced to devalue its currency in an effort to make its products more affordable. The global financial markets reacted badly and withdrew funds from Southeast Asia, throwing the whole region into decline. Billions of dollars were lost from the value of the economies.

ASIA'S RECOVERY

After millions of job losses and numerous company closures, the "Asian Tigers" are today on their way to pre-crisis levels of growth and prosperity. The recovery in Asia is being led by China and India. They managed to escape the Asian crisis and have now shown over a decade of consistent growth. The Indian economy expanded by an average of 5.7 percent a year between 1992 and 2002, and China's economy grew even faster at about 10 percent annually. This progress compares with annual growth in the United States and the United Kingdom of just 3.2 and 2.5 percent, respectively.

China's growth has focused on manufacturing industries. The service industry is also expanding rapidly, however, and China hopes to make Shanghai the financial center of Asia, replacing Tokyo and Hong Kong. Central to China's success has been its opening up to capitalist markets and allowing overseas companies to invest in China. China's engagement with the free market economy was most clearly indicated in 2001 when China joined the World Trade Organization (WTO)—the main global regulator of worldwide trade.

The Pudong District of Shanghai, China, was mainly agricultural land until 1990, but today it is at the heart of Shanghai's transformation into the financial capital of Asia.

Like China, India's economic growth has been due to a mix of both industry and services. India has developed particular strengths in the Information Technology (IT) industry, and it is now a major center for the global computer and software industry. Technological developments, such as the Internet and inexpensive international telephone rates, have also allowed India to become a world leader in the service sector. India is able to offer high-quality services at a much lower cost than in Europe, North America, or even eastern Asia. Several U.K. bank and insurance companies have transferred their call centers to India to take advantage of cost savings of about 40 percent. This employment practice is known as "offshoring" and has resulted in thousands of jobs moving to India from countries like the United States and the U.K.

A woman answers telephone calls in Bangalore, India, at one of the city's many call centers. This center handles calls relating to Texan insurance regulations and parts specifications for a U.S. automaker in Detroit.

TOURISM BOOM?

The economy of the Middle East is dominated by oil, but tourism is a fast growing sector. Israel has long attracted people who come to visit the Holy Land, but other key attractions include historic sites in Turkey and Jordan. Turkey has also benefited from coastal tourism along its beautiful Mediterranean beaches. Dubai, in the United Arab Emirates, has one of the fastest growing tourist sectors, which has developed around shopping, water sports, desert adventures, and luxury hotels. Between 1990 and 2003, the number of tourists visiting the Middle East increased from 10 to 28 million visitors per year. From 2001 to 2002 (a difficult time for the tourist industry in the wake of terrorist attacks in the United States), tourism in the Middle East grew by 17 percent—faster than in any other region of the world.

INFORMAL ECONOMY

Although Asian service sectors are expanding, many service jobs remain part of a vast informal economy—an unregulated, cash-based economy in which people normally pay little or no tax on their incomes. Typical services include portering, street vendors, rubbish collection, laundry services, and low-skilled manufacturing jobs. Recent studies have estimat-

The Mahalakshmi municipal dohbi ghats (open air laundries) in Mumbai, India, are a scene of frantic activity. Hundreds of dhobis (washermen and women) wash and dry thousands of articles of clothing every day as part of India's enormous informal economy. Services such as this are often performed by workers in the informal economy.

ed that the informal sector accounts for 67 to 78 percent of nonagricultural employment in Bangladesh, Pakistan, Thailand, Indonesia, and the Philippines. Women make up a disproportionate number in the informal sector because they are often prepared to work for less money. The textile industry in Asia is renowned for its use of low-paid female workers in the informal economic sector.

FACT FILE

Uzbekistan is the world's only double-landlocked country—it and all of its immediate neighboring countries are landlocked.

• • • • • • ➤ IN FOCUS: Rebuilding the Silk Road?

The original Silk Road is one of the oldest known trading routes in the world (dating to the Roman empire) and connected eastern China with markets in Europe, Africa, and the Middle East via a network of long-distance paths that crossed the Asian continent. Since 1996, there have been plans to rebuild the Silk Road as a future trade route. The idea originated in the former Soviet nations that occupy a region now commonly referred to as Central Asia (including Uzbekistan, Turkmenistan, and Azerbaijan). Since becoming independent of the Soviet Union, the economies of these countries have struggled to develop, hindered partly because they are extremely isolated from potential markets in Europe and eastern Asia. In addi-

tion, they inherited infrastructures (roads, rail networks, bridges, and so on) that were in a poor state of repair. A new Silk Road would bring economic benefits to Central Asia, opening up trade with the rest of the continent and with Europe to the west. It would also strengthen regional trade within Central Asia. The United Nations (UN), Asian Development Bank, European Union, and the U.S. government have all expressed support for the idea, because it would provide an export route for Central Asia's valuable energy resources.

A rugged section of the Karakoram Highway as it crosses from Pakistan into China. The Karakoram Highway is part of the famous Silk Road trade route that crosses the Asian continent.

7. ASIA IN THE WORLD

ASIA IS GEOGRAPHICALLY LOCATED BETWEEN THE TWO EXISTING world power centers of North America and Europe. This key position not only facilitates commerce and trade but also allows for the spread of ideas and cultural values. In the closing decades of the twentieth century, however, Asia has established itself as much more than a conveniently located continent. It is fast emerging as a major world power in and of itself, with strong and vibrant economies and a pivotal role in global politics. China and Russia, for example, have long been two of the five permanent members of the UN Security Council—the global body for ensuring peace and security in the world. Russia, along with Japan, is also a G8 country—a group of the world's eight most industrialized countries.

China and Russia hold permanent seats on the UN Security Council, meeting here at the United Nations headquarters in New York.

POWER FROM WITHIN

One of the most fundamental ways in which Asian countries influence the world is with the supply of crude oil—the basis of virtually all modern and energy-hungry economies. This influence is wielded through an organization called OPEC—the Organization of Petroleum Exporting Countries—that was formed in 1960. Its membership is made up of three African states (Libya, Algeria, and Nigeria), Venezuela in South America, and seven Asian countries (Saudi Arabia, Iran, Iraq, Kuwait, Indonesia, Qatar, and United Arab Emirates). Between them, they control about 80 percent of the world's oil reserves and about 40 percent of world oil production.

By having its members agree on production quotas, OPEC is able to alter the amount of oil entering the world markets and thereby influence global oil prices. This control was demonstrated most dramatically in 1973 when OPEC policies raised oil prices first by 70 percent and then again by a further 130 percent. Many countries faced major fuel shortages, while others accrued large debts as they struggled to buy fuel at the higher prices. So severe were the effects of the OPEC price increases that they have been blamed as a cause of the debt crises currently facing many of the world's poorer nations.

An intricate network of pipes forms part of the massive Ras Tanura oil refinery in Saudi Arabia. This country is a key member of OPEC, an organization able to influence the supply and price of the world's oil.

Some economists question whether OPEC is as powerful today as in the past because of the increase in oil supplied by non-OPEC members, including the United States, the UK, Mexico, Norway, and the Russian Federation. What is clear, however, is that OPEC demonstrated the significance of oil and, more specifically, Asian oil to world affairs. Its importance continues today and is often said to be at the heart of international interests in creating peace and stability in the Middle East and Central Asia. Lasting peace in the region would secure oil supplies and prices and, in doing so, bring greater stability to the global economy. In contrast, continued instability can cause fluctuating oil prices that have an impact on economies far removed from the region itself.

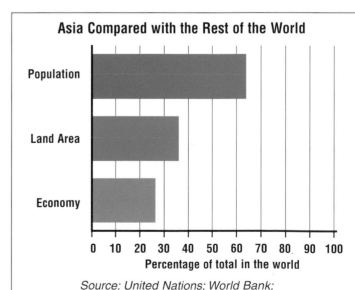

Asia Compared with the Rest of the World

Source: United Nations; World Bank;
Britannica Book of the Year 2004

GLOBAL HOTSPOTS

At the start of the twenty-first century, Asia has more hotspots than anywhere else in the world. These spots are places where conflict, tension, or instability threatens the lives of the people living there and, in some instances, those of a much wider area. Key hotspots include North Korea, Israel and the Palestinian territories, Afghanistan, Iraq, and Kashmir in northern India. Afghanistan and Iraq, for example, are struggling to rebuild after years of dictatorial rule by the Taliban in Afghanistan and Saddam Hussein in Iraq. These regimes ruled in a totalitarian and ruthless manner, abusing the human rights of their own citizens and often those of neighboring countries as well. Following the terrorist attacks in the United States on September 11th, 2001, links were made between the terrorists and the Taliban regime in Afghanistan. An international coalition led by the United States took military action to remove the Taliban as part of a global "war on terror," and the Taliban fell from power in December 2001.

An Iraqi man throws stones at a statue of Iraq president Saddam Hussein as it falls in central Baghdad, April 9, 2003. U.S. forces assisted Iraqi civilians in toppling the statue to symbolize the end of Saddam's regime. Democratic elections to elect a new interim government were held in Iraq in January 2005 .

The United States later led a campaign to remove Saddam Hussein from power in Iraq. His regime had used chemical weapons in the past, and concerns existed that such weapons of mass destruction (WMD) could fall into the hands of terrorists in the future. Many believed, therefore, that Iraq posed an immediate threat to U.S. security. The U.S.-led attack on Iraq brought about the collapse of Saddam Hussein's regime in April 2003. Although weapons of mass destruction were not found once the United States and its allies entered Iraq, both Iraq and

Afghanistan are now heading towards democratic self-governance. Tensions with opposing and rival groups, however, continue to boil over. International troops remain in Afghanistan and Iraq in an effort to maintain peace and security.

IN FOCUS: Israel, the Palestinians, and the Territories

Israel and Israeli-controlled territory that formerly made up the land called Palestine occupy a narrow slice of Asian land between the Mediterranean Sea and the Jordan River. For more than half a century, this land has been one of the most contested territories in the world, in large part because both Israel (which was founded in 1948 as a Jewish state) and Palestinian Arabs consider it to be their rightful homeland. A series of armed conflicts between Israel and its Arab neighbors in 1948, 1967, and 1973 saw Israel gain even greater control over the disputed territories. These gains included complete control over Jerusalem and important Muslim landmarks. An estimated 3.7 million Palestinians have been displaced as a result of these tensions and currently live in neighboring Arab countries and in the Israeli-controlled West Bank and Gaza Strip. Attempts to broker peace between Israel and the Palestinians have been led by the United States, but disagreements over control of Jerusalem and the return of Palestinian refugees have hampered progress. Talks have been further hampered by Jewish settlements in the West Bank and Gaza, Palestinian suicide bombings against Israeli targets, and Israeli military action in Palestinian areas. A new cease-fire and round of diplomatic talks between Israeli and Palestinian leaders in January 2005 have raised hopes for peace in the region.

A Palestinian youth throws a stone at Israeli soldiers during clashes in the center of the West Bank City of Ramallah.

51

North Korea is a country of particular concern to the international community because it has nuclear weapons that could be used against other countries. North Korea is one of the most isolated countries in the world and one of only a few remaining communist nations. Korea was divided in two in 1948, and North Korea has maintained a fragile cease-fire with South Korea since a war (1950–1953) between them ended. Governments around the world are concerned that North Korea could use its weapons if conflict were to resume. The international community is putting great pressure on North Korea to enter into talks to find a lasting peace for the Korean Peninsula. The U.S. government, along with China, Japan, Russia, and South Korea, are playing a key role in these negotiations.

WORLD DESTINATION

Asian influences in the areas of cuisine, cinema, design, philosophy, and religion, among others, have spread throughout the world and become part of daily life for people living well beyond the borders of the continent. The people of Asia themselves have also spread far and wide as evidenced by the number of Asian communities that have been established overseas. Many cities, including London, New York, Paris, and San Francisco, have their own "Chinatowns." Communities of immigrants from Bangladesh, India, Pakistan, Vietnam, Thailand, and many others can also be found in a wide range of countries.

The spread of Asian culture has, consequently, increased the desire of people to visit Asia themselves. Inexpensive airfares

The Great Wall of China is one of the major attractions drawing tourists to China, which will soon become the world's number one tourist destination.

A tourist approaches a group of Indian elephants at the Pinnawela Elephant Orphanage in Kegalle, Sri Lanka. Asia's wildlife is a key asset for its tourist industry.

and improved communications have made it easier to find out about and visit even extremely remote locations. High profile events, such as the World Cup (held in South Korea and Japan in 2002), have also helped boost Asia's appeal. In 2002, about 145 million tourists arrived in Asia, more than double the 62 million who visited in 1990. The top destinations were China (36.8 million), Hong Kong (16.6 million), Malaysia (13.3 million), and Thailand (10.9 million). China has a particularly thriving tourist industry and, in 2002, was ranked fifth in the world for both arrivals and income from tourism. China is also a becoming a significant generator of tourists itself as personal incomes rise and its population enjoys greater travel opportunities. This trend is significant for other Asian nations because travel within regions accounts for about 80 percent of all tourism. A further boost to China's tourist industry is expected when its capital, Beijing, hosts the Olympic Games in August 2008.

FACT FILE

By 2020, China is expected to become the world's leading tourist destination and the fourth-largest generator of tourists.

8. ASIAN WILDLIFE

*T*HE WILDLIFE OF ASIA IS EXTREMELY DIVERSE AND INCLUDES many unique species, such as the blind freshwater river dolphins of the Ganges, Yangtze, Indus, and Mekong rivers. Today, these animals are extremely endangered as a result of human interference or the destruction of their natural habitats. The same is true for much of Asia's other wildlife, including the Asian elephant, the Bengal and Siberian tigers, the Sumatran rhinoceros, and the giant panda in China.

A young giant panda plays on a tree in the Sichuan Province of China. Most of the 1,596 wild giant pandas recorded in 2004 live in the Sichuan Province. Their numbers have increased by 40 percent between 2000 and 2004 due to improved habitat conservation.

DECLINING HABITATS

The orangutan provides a good example of the dangers facing Asian wildlife. Orangutans (which means "people of the forest" in Malay) live in Indonesia and Malaysia, but deforestation for timber harvesting, agricultural land, or settlements has severely reduced their natural habitat. In 1900, about 318,000 orangutans lived in the wild but, today, fewer than 20,000 are thought to be left. Conservation experts believe the species may be disappearing at a rate of up to 2,000 animals per year. Orangutans face particular problems because their breeding cycle is very slow. Females do not begin to mate until about fifteen years of age and will wait about eight years between offspring—the longest period of parental care of any primate except humans. These delays mean the orangutan population reproduces itself very slowly. Indonesia has taken steps to try and protect orangutans by creating national parks, such as Tanjung Putting National Park formed in 1982. Policing these parks has proven difficult, however, and illegal logging remains widespread. Tanjung Putting alone is estimated to lose about US$8 million worth of timber every year.

PEOPLE AND WILDLIFE

One consequence of declining Asian habitats is that people and wildlife are increasingly brought into contact, with conflicts often the result. In 2002, a herd of about one hundred Asian elephants crossed into northern Bangladesh from Meghalaya state in India. The elephants migrated across the border when the forests they were living in were cleared for construction of a new highway. Crossing into Bangladesh, the elephants caused enormous damage to forests, homes, and crops and killed thirteen people, with many more injured. By late-2004, Bangladesh was threatening to kill the rampaging elephants unless they were returned to India. Although Bangladesh agreed that elephants should be protected, officials also stated that the animals could not be allowed to terrorize, injure, and kill local people. Between 1997 and mid-2004, about 180 people are known to have died in clashes with elephants across Bangladesh.

A young orangutan with its mother in Sumatra, Indonesia. Orangutans are threatened by human activities and economic development.

FACT FILE

Indonesia is one of the most species-rich countries in the world. It contains about 10 percent of the world's tropical rain forest, 17 percent of its bird species, 16 percent of reptile and amphibian species, and 12 percent of mammal species.

IN FOCUS: Project Tiger

One of Asia's most successful conservation examples is India's "Project Tiger." In 1900, India was home to an estimated 40,000 tigers, but a 1972 census recorded only 1,827 animals—a decline of more than 95 percent. Project Tiger was launched in 1973 to establish protected reserves in India's remaining tiger habitats and to enforce conservation of the species. Human activity was banned completely from the core of each reserve, although a buffer zone around each reserve has enabled local people to continue using the environment for their own needs, such as gathering fuelwood. Nine reserves were initially established in 1973–1974 and contained 268 tigers. The numbers have steadily increased to 27 reserves by 2003 with a protected population of 1,576 tigers. Project Tiger has attracted worldwide praise for its conservation work, and its reserves have become a major tourist attraction, with visitors paying large sums to see the largest of the world's cats. India launched "Project Elephant" in 1991–1992 to try and repeat the success of Project Tiger.

A group of tourists watch India's greatest predator, the tiger, in Bandhavgarh National Park, one of the parks involved in Project Tiger.

WORKING WITH WILDLIFE

Many of Asia's wild animals have been domesticated for human benefit. Elephants have long been used to move logs in the timber industry and also to serve as the centerpiece of many colorful festivals in India. Elephants are increasingly being used to provide rides or perform in shows for tourists, too. The use of elephants for this purpose, however, has been questioned. In 2000, a British tourist was killed in Thailand when a bull elephant performing during a show gouged her with his tusks. In desert regions, camels are used for transporting goods because they are ideally suited to the harsh desert environment. In India's desert city of Jaipur, camels are a regular feature of bustling city traffic. Buffalo or cattle are used by many Asian farmers to help plow the land, although this is declining as tractors become more widespread. A more unusual use of wildlife is found on the Yangtze river in China where fishermen use tamed cormorants to catch fish. These expert birds dive for fish from the edge of the boat and are prevented from swallowing the catch by a ring around their necks.

Owners give their camels a drink at the Pushkar Camel Fair in Rajasthan, in northern India. This annual camel fair is the world's largest and draws thousands of traders and their valued animals. Camels are still used for transporting goods in Rajasthan.

FACT FILE

In May 2004, a new flightless bird species, named the Calayan rail (*Gallirallus calayanensis*), was discovered in the forests of Calayan, an island in the Philippines.

9. THE FUTURE OF ASIA

AT THE START OF THE TWENTY-FIRST CENTURY, ASIA IS A continent on the brink of realizing its full potential. Its economies are growing well, its people are healthier and better educated than ever before, and it is playing an extremely important role in world affairs. Led by the emerging powers of China and India, and under the existing influence of Japan and the "tiger economies," Asia can look ahead with great optimism to the future.

South Korean border guards patrol the demilitarized zone (DMZ) that has separated South and North Korea since 1953 and which remains the last Cold War frontier in Asia.

REGIONAL STRENGTH

One of Asia's greatest benefits is its regional strength. Between them, Asian nations control a significant percentage of the world's resources, and they also share the largest potential market for finished products. As incomes rise, it is expected that Asian countries will increasingly look to trade within the region and become less dependent on their historical markets in Europe and North America. If plans such as the rebuilding of the Great Silk Road are realized, then intraregional trading will be further strengthened.

STABILITY AND PEACE

Of vital importance to the future of the continent is an end to the conflicts and tensions that have plagued some parts of Asia for more than half a century. The tense relationship between North and South Korea, for example, was heightened in 2005 by the revelation that North Korea possessed nuclear weapons. The Israeli/Palestinian conflict also remains unresolved despite U.S. and international pressure to steer the two parties toward a road map for peace. In addition, the need to help rebuild the lives of those in Afghanistan and Iraq affected by years of instability and conflict is pressing following the overthrow of the brutal regimes in those countries in 2001 and 2003, respectively. For people so used to violence and internal conflict, becoming a stable and peaceful society is a continuing struggle. The international community is concerned that a failure to bring about peace in these troubled parts of Asia could spawn more terrorist groups, such as al-Qaeda.

SUSTAINABLE DEVELOPMENT

Meeting the needs of its massive population without further degrading its natural environments will be a key challenge for Asia's future. This challenge is one of sustainable development. Issues such as habitat destruction, overuse of resources, and pollution are already serious concerns for large parts of the continent. The fear is that as incomes and living standards rise and approach those of North America or Western Europe, these issues will become increasingly more serious. The number of cars in China, for instance, has more than doubled from just 5.8 million in 1990 to more than 13 million by 2002, bringing associated problems of pollution with them. One thing is clear—the continent that witnessed the dawn of the world's first civilizations will play a major role in determining the direction and sustainability of those in the future.

China's booming economy has created new problems, such as road congestion and pollution, as shown here in Beijing. Overcoming such problems is vital to the sustainable development of the country.

STATISTICAL COMPENDIUM

Nation	Area (sq miles)	Population (2003)	Urbanization (% population) 2003	Life expectancy at birth 2002 (in years)	GDP per capita (US$) 2002	Percentage of population under 15 years 2003	Percentage of population over 65 years 2003
Afghanistan	251,759	23,897,000	23.3	43.0	N/A	44	3
Armenia	11,481	3,061,000	64.4	72.3	3,120	20	10
Azerbaijan	33,428	8,370,000	50.0	72.1	3,210	27	7
Bahrain	268	724,000	90.0	73.9	17,170	27	3
Bangladesh	56,962	146,736,000	24.2	61.1	1,700	35	3
Bhutan	18,142	2,257,000	8.5	63.0	1,969	42	4
Brunei	2,225	358,000	76.2	76.2	19,210	30	3
Cambodia	70,220	14,144,000	18.6	57.4	2,060	39	3
China	3,695,139	1,304,196,000	38.6	70.9	4,580	24	7
Georgia	26,824	5,126,000	51.9	73.5	2,260	18	14
Hong Kong	422	7,049,000	100.0	79.9	26,910	16	12
India	1,221,920	1,065,462,000	28.3	63.7	2,670	32	5
Indonesia	747,751	219,883,000	45.6	66.6	3,230	29	5
Iran	635,070	68,920,000	66.7	70.1	6,690	29	5
Iraq	167,930	25,175,000	67.2	63.0	N/A	39	3
Israel	7,844	6,433,000	91.6	79.1	19,530	27	10
Japan	145,838	127,654,000	65.4	81.5	26,940	14	19
Jordan	34,480	5,473,000	79.0	70.9	4,220	37	3
Kazakhstan	1,051,811	15,433,000	55.8	66.2	5,870	25	8
Korea, North	47,386	22,664,000	61.1	63.0	N/A	26	7
Korea, South	38,317	47,700,000	80.3	75.4	16,950	21	8
Kuwait	6,878	2,521,000	96.3	76.5	16,240	25	2
Kyrgyzstan	77,161	5,138,000	33.9	68.4	1,620	32	6
Laos	91,405	5,657,000	20.7	54.3	1,720	42	3
Lebanon	4,014	3,653,000	87.5	73.5	4,360	30	6
Macau	8	464,000	98.9	79.0	N/A	21	7
Malaysia	127,277	24,425,000	63.9	73.0	9,120	33	4
Maldives	44	318,000	28.8	67.2	4,798	39	4
Mongolia	603,749	2,594,000	56.7	63.7	1,710	32	4
Myanmar	261,159	49,485,000	29.4	57.2	1,027	32	4
Nepal	56,812	25,164,000	15.0	59.6	1,370	40	4
Occupied Palestinian Territory	2,418	3,557,000	71.1	72.3	N/A	45	3
Oman	119,467	2,851,000	77.6	72.3	13,340	41	3
Pakistan	307,293	153,578,000	34.1	60.8	1,940	40	3
Philippines	115,829	79,999,000	61.0	69.8	4,170	36	4
Qatar	4,415	610,000	92.0	72.0	19,844	24	3
Russia	6,591,104	143,246,000	73.3	66.7	8,230	16	13

Saudi Arabia	867,728	24,217,000	87.7	72.1	12,650	40	3
Singapore	249	4,253,000	100.0	78.0	24,040	21	8
Sri Lanka	25,325	19,065,000	21.0	72.5	3,570	25	7
Syria	71,479	17,800,000	50.1	71.7	3,620	38	3
Tajikistan	55,237	6,245,000	24.7	68.6	980	36	5
Thailand	198,062	62,833,000	31.9	69.1	7,010	23	7
Timor-Leste	N/A	778,000	7.6	49.3	N/A	40	N/A
Turkey	300,868	71,325,000	66.3	70.4	6,390	28	6
Turkmenistan	188,407	4,867,000	45.3	66.9	4,300	34	4
United Arab Emirates	32,270	2,995,000	85.1	74.6	22,420	19	2
Uzbekistan	172,696	26,093,000	36.6	69.5	1,670	34	5
Vietnam	127,782	81,377,000	25.7	69.0	2,300	30	5
Yemen	214,230	20,010,000	25.6	59.8	870	45	3

Sources: UN Agencies, World Bank, and Britannica

GLOSSARY

chaebol a group of companies in South Korea that operate in different fields but are all part of one parent company. The largest chaebols have evolved from family-run businesses.

cold war the conflict between the differing political and economic ideologies of capitalist democracies (led by the United States) and socialist communists (led by the former USSR), which dominated world politics between 1945 and 1990

deforestation the removal of forest trees and vegetation; being cleared of forests

feng-shui the Chinese practice of placing, configuring, or arranging a building, room, or space in such a way as to harmonize the flow of energy within that space

groundwater water that is held in porous rocks and soils in the ground

HIV/AIDS Human Immunodeficiency Virus (HIV) is a deadly virus spread by unprotected sex or contaminated needles or blood supplies. It can develop into Acquired Immuno-Defiency Syndrome (AIDS), which is fatal. Expensive drugs can keep people alive, but there is no cure.

homo sapiens sapiens the scientific name of modern human beings

hydroelectric power (HEP) a type of energy generated by fast-flowing water flowing through turbines

independence the quality or state of having self-governance rather than being under the control of others; when a country wins the right to control its own affairs

infant mortality the number of babies, out of every thousand born, who die before the age of one

infrastructure the systems and public works that allow communication and/or help people and the economy to function, including roads, railroads, electricity, and phone lines

Islamic of or relating to the faith of Islam, such as Islamic buildings or designs

maritime of, relating to, or bordering on the ocean or sea; of or relating to shipping, sailing, or commerce on the sea

origami the Japanese art of folding squares of paper into the shapes of objects or things

partition the process by which the Indian Subcontinent was divided into modern-day India, Pakistan, and Bangladesh following independence from Britain in 1948

population momentum the process by which a population continues to grow in absolute numbers even when the rate of growth has slowed. The continued growth is normally due to a large proportion of the population yet to enter child-bearing age.

service sector the part of the economy that provides services such as banking and retail

urbanization the process of a region or country becoming urbanized, meaning that its population increasingly lives in urban areas (towns or cities)

FURTHER INFORMATION

BOOKS TO READ:

Barber, Nicola. *Beijing*. Great Cities of the World (series). Milwaukee: World Almanac Library, 2004.

Cumming, David. *The Ganges*. Great Rivers of the World (series). Milwaukee: World Almanac Library, 2003.

Fiscus, James W. *America's War in Afghanistan*. War and Conflict in the Middle East. New York: Rosen Publishing, 2004.

Kazem, Halima. *Afghanistan*. Countries of the World (series). Milwaukee: Gareth Stevens, 2003.

Netzley, Patricia D. *Japan*. Modern Nations of the World (series). San Diego: Lucent Books, 2000.

Waterlow, Julia. *The Yangtze*. Great Rivers of the World (series). Milwaukee: World Almanac Library, 2003.

USEFUL WEB SITES:

www.asia-art.net/index.html
Read about the histories and techniques of several Asian art forms, from Chinese brush painting and Japanese ceramics to Indonesian batik and Vietnamese silk paintings.

www.geographyiq.com/asia.htm
GeographyIQ provides quick facts, maps, background information, and commentary for countries in Asia and the other continents.

library.thinkquest.org/10131/
Destination Himalayas is a site that lets you discover the highest point on Earth. Learn about these majestic mountains, what it takes to climb to the top, the lands that surround them, their geological past, and the plants and animals that live there.

INDEX

ABOUT THE AUTHOR

Rob Bowden is a freelance author and photographer specializing in geographical and environmental issues and with a particular interest in less developed regions. He has made several trips to research and photograph books in Asia, including, most recently, India and South Korea. He has also lectured in geography and development studies at Sussex, Brighton, and Keele universities in the United Kingdom.